REDISCOVERING

JOY

SEEKING GOD'S PRESENCE
IN EVERY MOMENT

31 Devotions to Strengthen Your Faith and Cultivate a Deeper Relationship with God

JASMINE CHIKARA

DEDICATION

This devotional is dedicated to my beloved grandfather, Elbert, whom I will always hold close to my heart. The loss of my grandfather to lung cancer was undoubtedly one of the darkest periods of my life. I found myself consumed by feelings of isolation that led me to distance myself from those around me. The grieving process was overwhelming, and I struggled to find a way to cope. There were days when simply getting out of bed seemed like an insurmountable task, and I was sinking into a state of depression. However, my life took a turn when I started incorporating prayer, meditation, and daily devotions into my routine.

Gradually, I began to feel less alone. I attribute this newfound solace to the practice of reading devotionals and the unwavering support of my loved ones. By seeking solace in God, I was filled with hope and found the strength to believe that I would overcome this dark period in my life.

I pray this devotional will be a guiding light to help you navigate through any troubles that may be burdening your heart at this time. May you find solace, comfort, and guidance in the Lord. Remember, you are capable of persevering through even the most challenging times.

CONTENTS

Acknowledgments vii

Note from the Author .ix

Day 1   You Are Not Alone 1

Day 2   Don't Worry 4

Day 3   Trust in God 7

Day 4   Fearless 10

Day 5   Follow God's Plan 13

Day 6   Live Stress-Free 16

Day 7   It Is Written 20

Day 8   Develop Your Gifts 24

Day 9   Find Strength in God 28

Day 10   Protected 31

Day 11   Gratefulness 34

Day 12   Don't Be Discouraged 37

Day 13   Keep Doing the Right Things 40

Day 14   Seek God for Direction 43

Day 15 The Armor of God 46

Day 16 Be Strong 49

Day 17 Joy 53

Day 18 God Is with You 56

Day 19 Faith 60

Day 20 Forgiveness 64

Day 21 Humility in the Battle 67

Day 22 God's Approval 70

Day 23 Let Your Light Shine 74

Day 24 God Will Supply Your Needs 77

Day 25 Be Thankful. 80

Day 26 Be of Good Cheer. 84

Day 27 Words Are Powerful 87

Day 28 Resist Temptation. 91

Day 29 Unconditional Love 95

Day 30 Perseverance 99

Day 31 Name Change. 102

About the Author .105

ACKNOWLEDGMENTS

I thank my parents, Brenda and Lonnie, for their dedication and guidance throughout this process. I would also like to thank my siblings—Bria, LJ, and Brooks, for their unwavering support and love. They helped me see this project to the end and reminded me of my greatness, even when I didn't always see it in myself. Your love is unmatched, and I cherish each of you eternally.

To Bishop Larry Minor and Prophetess Barbara Minor, thank you for your spiritual guidance and wisdom. I love you both endlessly. Your ministry has strengthened my faith and filled me with the Word of God.

NOTE FROM THE AUTHOR

I became inspired to write this devotional to encourage those experiencing grief, adversity, and hopelessness. Each devotion is intended to provide profound clarity and reflection on Scripture, accompanied by a prayer to recite throughout your day. I hope that these scriptures resonate deeply within your spirit. I also encourage you to take time for introspection and write in the reflection section at the end of your day or immediately after reading the devotional.

Please share this devotional with your friends and family. My prayer is that you find healing and encouragement on your journey. It is time to reclaim your joy! May God's peace surround and comfort you. You are a warrior, an amazing gift from God. Remember, He has chosen you as His child and showered you with His unfailing love!

DAY 1

YOU ARE NOT ALONE

"Don't be afraid, for I am with you. Don't be discouraged,
for I am your God. I will strengthen you and help you.
I will hold you up with my victorious right hand."
ISAIAH 41:10 NLT

Oh, what a wonderful friend we have in Jesus! At times in my life, I felt lost and afraid. I lacked confidence in myself and felt alone. However, God's love for me has always brought me comfort. When we walk with God, we are never alone. He protects and comforts us, serving as our strength and refuge. God sees every tear that falls from our eyes and every lonely night we endure. He is the source of peace, not confusion. Take solace in His Word and invite His presence into your surroundings.

May your spirit be uplifted and your faith restored. Even when you can't comprehend your circumstances, your heavenly Father is there to balance the scales. Let His perfect peace permeates your heart. His Word encourages you; you are a child of the Most High God. There is no reason to fear.

PRAYER

Father, at this moment, I feel weak and afraid. Please help me to see myself as You see me. I am more than a conqueror; You have given me the grace I need to handle anything that comes my way. Thank You for restoring my peace and allowing me to walk in Your light. In Jesus' name, we pray. Amen.

REFLECTION

In what ways have you experienced God's protection, comfort, and strength as you walk with Him?

_____

_____

_____

_____

_____

_____

_____

_____

How does knowing that He sees your tears and understands your loneliness bring you solace?

_____

_____

_____

_____

_____

_____

_____

_____

_____

DAY 2

DON'T WORRY

"Therefore, do not worry about tomorrow, for tomorrow will worry about itself. Each day has enough trouble of its own."
MATTHEW 6:34 NIV

We often find ourselves consumed by concern over our future and how things will unfold, leading to unnecessary worry and stress. However, I have good news to share: God doesn't want you to worry. He desires for you to find rest, knowing that He is working all things together for your good (Romans 8:28).

Instead of being preoccupied with the future, focus on the gift of today and embrace the present moment. Life is fleeting, and what you're currently worrying about can be resolved through God's answer to your prayers in a matter of hours, days, or months.

Trusting in God's ways, which are beyond our understanding, can bring greater peace. Our own clever plans and logic pale in comparison to God's supernatural favor in our lives. He has the ability to make the impossible possible. By resting in the assurance that God is more than capable of meeting all our needs, we can let go of worrying. While it's important to do what we can, when we can to the best of our abilities, we should also allow God to take care of the rest.

Let us not waste another moment of worry. Trust in God's providence; stay present and have faith that He is working for our good.

PRAYER

Father, thank You for loving me so much that You don't want me to worry. Let me cast all my cares and worries unto You. I know You have an excellent plan for my life. I surrender it all to You. In Jesus' name, we pray. Amen.

REFLECTION

Consider instances in your life where you have witnessed God's supernatural favor and His ability to make the impossible possible. How does reflecting on these moments strengthen your faith and alleviate worry?

_____

_____

_____

_____

_____

_____

_____

In your prayers, how can you specifically surrender your worries and cast your cares unto God?

_____

_____

_____

_____

_____

_____

_____

_____

DAY 3

TRUST IN GOD

"Trust in the LORD with all your heart and lean not on your understanding; in all your ways submit to him, and he will make your paths straight."

PROVERBS 3: 5-6 NIV

Refusing to rely on your understanding and submitting your ways to God is easier said than done. Sometimes your paths may not be apparent, and you must solely depend on God to guide you. It's crucial to always put your faith in the Lord and trust that He knows every detail of your life. Even when His plans don't make sense to you, remember that He knows what's best for you. His ways surpass yours in greatness and wisdom. He holds the master plan.

When the Israelites journeyed to the Promise Land, God purposely made them take the long route—the Bible says in a "roundabout" way (Exodus 13:17-18). He did so because He knew about the significant obstacles that lay ahead of them. These obstacles may have caused the Israelites to give up before reaching their destinies. God knew the Israelites would need to overcome the battle within their minds and build their faith muscles to prosper in the Promise Land.

God extends the same unfailing love to us as He did the Israelites, even when they displayed ungratefulness and uncertainty about His plan. He cares too deeply for you to let you miss your destiny. Therefore, make it a priority to seek Him today. Rest assured that He will not lead you astray. May His peace envelop and comfort you as you navigate life.

PRAYER

Father, our hearts are heavy; please comfort us with Your unfailing love. You are the light unto my feet. Illuminate the darkness and reveal the path I should take. I open my heart to receive You. Release any negative thoughts in my mind. Break every barrier and chain that tries to block me from reaching my destiny. I trust in You and seek Your divine direction as I move through this day. In Jesus' Name, we pray. Amen.

REFLECTION

Take a moment to envision God's light illuminating your path and breaking every chain that holds you back from reaching your destiny. How does this imagery inspire you to trust Him more fully?

_____

_____

_____

_____

_____

_____

_____

How does the verse from Proverbs 3:5-6 inspire you to trust in the Lord with all your heart and submit to His guidance, even when you don't fully understand His ways?

_____

_____

_____

_____

_____

_____

_____

DAY 4

FEARLESS

"For God did not give us a spirit of fear. He gave us a spirit of power and of love and of a good mind."
2 TIMOTHY 1:7 NLV

Fear can be paralyzing if we let it. It sneaks up on us, and we begin to second-guess ourselves; it's a stronghold that can be hard to break.

My battle with anxiety started at a young age. I remember memorizing today's scripture and reciting it daily to find the strength to overcome my fears. But I know that God didn't give us the spirit of fear! Don't let the Enemy trick you into believing his lies. Acknowledge your fears and ask God for the strength to overcome them.

Let nothing come between you and your dreams. As the saying goes, feel the fear and do it anyway. Your biggest miracle might be on the other side of fear. So, step into it and witness God working through you. He bestows a fresh anointing that commands your fears to lose their grip.

Remember, when you overcome your fears, you're not just doing it for yourself. Think about your children or the generations coming after you who will experience freedom because you decided to break a curse and embrace the unknown boldly. Someone else's destiny can be unlocked because you have the courage to walk in your truth and let go of your fears. Fearlessly being yourself is the best gift you can offer to this world. Take a step forward to receive God's unfailing love and infinite glory!

PRAYER

Father, I no longer want to wrestle with my fears. You have given me the power to overcome them. Please help me to live freely and be true to myself, using my gifts to enrich Your kingdom. I am no longer a slave to fear! In Jesus' name, we pray. Amen.

REFLECTION

According to 2 Timothy 1:7, what did God give us instead of a spirit of fear? How does this truth empower you to face your fears?

_____

_____

_____

_____

_____

_____

Reflect on the saying, "Feel the fear and do it anyway." In what areas of your life do you feel fear holding you back? How can you overcome those fears and trust God to work through you?

_____

_____

_____

_____

_____

_____

DAY 5

FOLLOW GOD'S PLAN

"For I know the plans I have for you," declares the LORD, "plans to prosper you and not to harm you, plans to give you hope and a future."
JEREMIAH 29:11 NIV

Don't be too quick to try to plan every detail of your life. I understand this may be challenging for those who, like me, are super organized, detail-oriented, "Type A" personalities. I can't even begin to count the number of nights I spent worrying about events that hadn't happened yet. By the time I turned 18, I had already created a timeline of how I thought my life should unfold, meticulously planning the when, what age, and how it would all happen. Let me tell you; I'm quite certain that God was probably laughing at me, thinking, "My daughter thinks she's in control and knows what's best."

As time went by, I started to see myself achieving my goals and realizing that everything didn't go according to plan. I had to let go of my timeline and reconnect with the ultimate planner, God. I held onto this scripture when doubt filled my mind and distressed me. I knew that no matter what detours arose, they were still part of God's perfect plan to guide me to where I was meant to be, fulfilling His promise to give me hope and a future.

Find rest in God's perfect peace and surrender to His will. He will bless your life in ways you never imagined!

PRAYER

Father, we know Your ways are far better than ours. Comfort us with Your Holy Spirit when we are overcome with doubt and worry. Let us know that Your plans for our lives will always prevail and lead us to peace and harmony. I trust You to make a way when I don't see a way. I will always give You glory for all You do. In Jesus' name, we pray. Amen.

REFLECTION

Reflect on a specific moment when you realized your life didn't go according to your planned timeline. How did it impact your trust in God's guidance and His perfect plan?

_____

_____

_____

_____

_____

_____

_____

_____

How does the verse from Jeremiah 29:11 assure us of God's plans for our lives?

_____

_____

_____

_____

_____

_____

_____

_____

DAY 6

LIVE STRESS-FREE

*"Cast your cares on the LORD and he will sustain
you; he will never let the righteous be shaken."*

PSALM 55: 22 NIV

Sometimes the demands of life weigh heavily on our spirits. We try our best to fix things, but we often forget to invite God into the issues that concern us. I, too, was so busy trying to keep up with a schedule and get things done that I became overwhelmed with all the tasks. In those moments of heaviness and stress, it is crucial to learn how to call on Jesus. When the load becomes too heavy to bear, we must remember that we are not alone and ask God for guidance.

It is not enough to simply ask God for advice; we must also be willing to utilize the tools and resources He sends to help us. How many times do we need assistance but allow pride to prevent us from reaching out and asking for help? We may even consider ourselves modest by declining assistance in order to maintain a sense of strength. However, this mindset only leads to stress, weariness, stagnation, and reduced creativity.

Certain tasks in our lives require us to engage in community and work with a team of like-minded individuals to make progress and enrich God's kingdom. We see this in Exodus 18:14-23 when Moses' father-in-law Jethro asks, "What are you trying to accomplish here? Why are you trying to do all this alone... You're going to wear yourself out... This job is too heavy a burden for you to handle all by yourself."

Jethro recognized that for Moses to fulfill his tasks without the limitations of worry, he would need the help of others. Consequently, Moses began to delegate tasks to others, relieving his stress and becoming a more effective leader.

We were never meant to have all the answers or navigate life alone. Surrender your concerns to God and accept the blessing of help when it is offered. I promise you things will get better.

PRAYER

Father, I surrender this day to You and release all stress. Come into my heart and renew my spirit. Please give me the strength to walk away from things I cannot control and allow You to work in my life. I know everything is working together for my good, and I will not be shaken. You have all the tools and resources lined up that I will need to accomplish my goals and prosper. Father, I will magnify You and not my problems. Please remove the stress that burdens me and bring my spirit peace and calmness. In Jesus' name, we pray. Amen.

REFLECTION

How do you remember to invite God into the overwhelming issues of your life and seek His guidance?

_____

_____

_____

_____

_____

_____

_____

_____

What steps can you take to overcome pride and ask for help from both God and others when faced with burdens and challenges?

_____

_____

_____

_____

_____

_____

_____

_____

DAY 7

IT IS WRITTEN

"And the Lord answered me, and said, Write the vision, and make it plain upon tables, that he may run that readeth it. For the vision is yet for an appointed time, but at the end it shall speak, and not lie: though it tarry, wait for it; because it will surely come, it will not tarry."

HABAKKUK 2:2-3 KJV

I am a firm believer in the power of writing down a plan. There is something about declaring a dream, putting it into writing, and then surrendering it to God. However, it's important to remember that a dream only works if we do; we need a blueprint.

That blueprint serves as a compass that guides us when we feel like giving up. It reminds us that no matter how long it takes, we have a plan and are committed to doing everything we can to make it happen.

When I turned 25, I wrote down my goal of owning my first home by the time I turned 30. I ensured my finances were in order and gained independence by moving out of my parent's home and getting an apartment. I faced numerous doubts and negative thoughts, questioning whether I could buy and maintain a home independently. The housing market was challenging, with a seller's market, housing shortages, and bidding wars due to the pandemic. I honestly had doubts about whether it would ever happen.

When my apartment lease was up, I decided not to renew it because I knew in my heart that God had called me to home-ownership. I returned home to live with my parents and regrouped. I revised my plan, giving myself 3-6 months to find a home and narrowing down the areas I wanted to live in. I began my search again, and by the grace of God, I put a contract on a home in December 2021 and closed on it within the time frame I had written down. This is just one example of the countless blessings God has bestowed upon my life.

I genuinely believe that every goal or vision God has placed in my heart will come to pass. When I write my plans out to

God, I make them clear and specific. However, I also submit those plans to Him, acknowledging that His will shall be done. I am also open to His blessings in whatever way He sees fit. I hold my plans loosely and remain close to God's plan for my life.

If your dreams have not yet come to pass, don't worry. Keep doing what is right, honoring God, and trust that you will reap a bountiful harvest in due time.

PRAYER

Father, You know the desires of my heart and the dreams that live inside me. Please give me the faith to keep believing in my vision, even when I see no progress. For I know the testing of my faith develops my character. I will have patience and meditate on Your Word while waiting for the vision to come to pass. Your Word does not return void but gives everlasting life. In Jesus' name, we pray. Amen.

REFLECTION

How can writing down your dreams and goals, and surrendering them to God, impact your journey?

_____

_____

_____

_____

_____

_____

_____

_____

_____

How can you maintain trust in God's timing while actively working toward your goals?

_____

_____

_____

_____

_____

_____

_____

_____

DAY 8

DEVELOP YOUR GIFTS

"A man's gift makes room for him
and brings him in front of great men."
PROVERBS 18:16 NLV

Each of us possesses a unique gift to offer the world. Some of us are aware of our gifts, while others are still discovering them. It is often the things we do effortlessly that bring us true fulfillment. We never tire of fulfilling our calling or living out our purpose.

When God has a specific plan for your life, you cannot escape it or be separated from it; that gift will always reside within you. Even if it lies dormant for a while, it will eventually find a way to manifest itself.

At times, we may feel unsure of how to bring our dreams to fruition and find ourselves losing focus amidst our daily routines. Let me assure you that it is imperative to honor and fulfill your gift. Every action you take at this very moment is leading you back to your purpose. You may ask, "But my life is so hectic, how will I ever find the time to pursue my dreams?" It is crucial to carve out time and create space to perfect your craft. Your gift was placed within you to unlock your destiny and, above all, to bless the kingdom of God.

If you find yourself going in circles, pause and reassess whether you are aligning with your purpose. Be courageous enough to release anything that holds you back. Pursuing your purpose will bring a higher level of fulfillment, something that money alone cannot buy. Begin each day with small steps, gradually building momentum toward achieving your purpose. Your gift will create opportunities, open doors, and place you in situations you never imagined. It's time to stop running and fully utilize the gift within you.

PRAYER

Father, help me to follow my dreams and use the gifts You've given me even when they scare me. I believe my gifts will make room for me and give me a platform to be used for Your glory. Please provide me with discipline in cultivating my gifts. I know what You have promised me shall come to pass. In Jesus' name, we pray. Amen.

REFLECTION

What obstacles or fears prevent you from fully utilizing your gift? How can you overcome them?

_____

_____

_____

_____

_____

_____

_____

_____

How can you use your gift to bless the kingdom of God and serve others?

_____

_____

_____

_____

_____

_____

_____

_____

_____

DAY 9

FIND STRENGTH IN GOD

"I can do all things through Christ that strengthens me."
PHILIPPIANS 4: 13 NKJV

Today's scripture is my favorite and the first one I memorized. If there is one scripture that the world knows, it's this one! Whenever I feel defeated or uncertain, this scripture comes to mind.

We all have our own giants to confront. Life can hit us hard and throw unexpected challenges our way, making us feel as if we can't recover. But when God breathes life into us, we have no choice but to persevere.

What the Enemy intends for harm, God can turn around for our benefit. David defeated the giant Goliath. No one saw it coming, but God knew David was prepared for the battle. When the Enemy attacked him with power, David fought back with the unmatched Word of God, which gave him the strength to overcome the giant and emerge victorious. Consider your own life. What giants stand in your path? Have you prayed and asked God to deliver you from them? Remember, with God, all things are possible (Matthew 19:26). God is the great I AM, capable of being whatever you need in your life. Regain your strength and know that God is with you. He will guide you through every challenge you face.

PRAYER

Father, I command every doubt and fear to be removed from my thoughts. Through Christ, You have made me strong, and I am more than a conqueror. I believe in what Your Word says about me and not in the negative opinions of others. You have given me the strength to triumph through adversity and succeed. I will follow Your plan and become who You have called me to be. In Jesus' name, we pray. Amen.

REFLECTION

Reflecting on your own life, how has persevering through difficult times helped you grow and strengthen your faith?

_____

_____

_____

_____

_____

_____

_____

How can you actively seek guidance from God to overcome the giants in your path?

_____

_____

_____

_____

_____

_____

_____

_____

DAY 10

PROTECTED

"No weapon formed against you shall prosper, and every tongue which rises against you in judgment you shall condemn. This is the heritage of the servants of the Lord, and their righteousness is from Me," Says the Lord."

ISAIAH 54:17 NKJV

When it's time for spiritual warfare, I make sure to have this scripture at hand! If you think following Christ is all about cuteness and fun, think again. The moment you surrendered your life to God, the Devil began plotting ways to attack you. He knows your weaknesses and will exploit them. It's not a comfortable topic to discuss, but the Enemy does possess power. But let me share a secret with you: the Enemy's power pales in comparison to God's power and His love for His children. So, when those weapons are formed against you—and trust me, they will—understand that they may cause irritation or hurt your feelings, but they will not succeed. Once you pray and stand firmly on God's Word, the Devil's plans for your life are canceled. Walk boldly in the power God has bestowed upon you!

If God has given you authority to speak to the mountains in your life and see them removed, maintain that same energy when it comes to the Devil and his wicked schemes. Let him know that you are a child of the Most High God, covered by the blood of Jesus. You will not be shaken or cower in fear because the presence of the Lord is with you!

PRAYER

Father, the weapons have formed against me, and I am on the battleground. I know Your light tramples the darkness, and I will remain anchored to Your Word. I rebuke any assignment the Enemy has on my life and remain fervent in prayer. For Your Word breathes life into me and renews my spirit. I will be victorious over the Enemy's schemes and exalt Your mighty name. Thank You, Jesus! In Jesus' name, we pray. Amen.

REFLECTION

Have you experienced moments when the Devil tried to attack you or exploit your weaknesses? How did you respond?

_____

_____

_____

_____

_____

_____

_____

_____

How does knowing that God's Word promises protection against weapons impact your perspective on spiritual warfare?

_____

_____

_____

_____

_____

_____

_____

_____

DAY 11

GRATEFULNESS

"Surely goodness and mercy shall follow me all the days of my life: and I will dwell in the house of the Lord forever."

PSALM 23:6 KJV

When we wake up, it is important to be grateful for the simple things. The fact that you are still here and God has promised His goodness and mercy will follow you all the days of your life is enough to make you shout praises to His Holy name! Before allowing negative thoughts to enter your mind, remember that God breathed new life into you.

You are here for a purpose, and He chose you! Yes, He chose you, even when you didn't choose Him. That's how much God loves you. He causes His face to shine down on you. Regardless of your circumstances or how far you may have fallen, there is joy and hope to be found in His Word. God's grace is always sufficient, for His power is made strong in weakness (2 Corinthians 12:19). Continue seeking God, and you will find Him. He will reveal Himself in subtle ways. Stay in tune with your spirit, and let God guide you. Even when you feel undeserving, God yearns to be good to you. That's His everlasting and all-powerful mercy and goodness in our lives. Receive it with an open heart!

PRAYER

Father, we come to You with a heart full of gratitude, thanking You for the day. We know not what this day may bring, but we can overcome anything with You. We open our hearts to receive Your unfailing love and compassion. Something good is going to happen to us today! Thank You for Your provision and protection. Please continue to cover us with Your grace. In Jesus' name, we pray. Amen.

REFLECTION

Reflect on a time when you experienced God's provision and protection. How does that memory strengthen your faith?

_____

_____

_____

_____

_____

_____

How does the knowledge of God's grace being sufficient in your weakness bring you comfort?

_____

_____

_____

_____

_____

_____

_____

_____

DAY 12

DON'T BE DISCOURAGED

*"And we know that all things work together for good
to them that love God, to them
who are the called according to his purpose."*
ROMANS 8:28 KJV

Our lives are full of twists and turns. Things may happen that we don't understand, but one thing we know for sure is that God is directing our steps. Even when things don't go as planned, we can place our complete confidence in Him. You may be going through something so painful right now that you question God's presence, or you may ask, "God, if You love me, why would You allow this painful experience to happen?"

Following God does not exempt us from painful experiences; sometimes, we may encounter periods of sadness or disappointment. However, we must remember that this pain is not permanent. We must endure it and remain rooted in God's Word. We should seek the lesson that God is trying to reveal and understand that even heartbreak, failure, or trauma can be used for our good, propelling us toward our purpose and leading us to God's destiny.

So, the next time you face a setback or feel discouraged, remember that the struggle won't last forever. You serve a big God who has an even bigger plan for your life. In time, you will reflect on what once held you back and see it as a bridge that carried you to a greater purpose.

PRAYER

Father, console me in the way You do that takes away my fears and pain. I am in a season where nothing seems to be going my way, but I trust Your ways are far greater than mine. This setback and hurt can be used for my good to propel me forward. Give me the strength to endure this season with a grateful heart and a positive attitude. I trust in You always. In Jesus' name, we pray. Amen.

REFLECTION

Reflect on a past experience where you eventually saw how a setback or pain propelled you forward. How did that realization impact your faith?

_____

_____

_____

_____

_____

_____

_____

How can you cultivate a grateful heart and a positive attitude in the midst of a challenging season?

_____

_____

_____

_____

_____

_____

_____

DAY 13

KEEP DOING THE RIGHT THINGS

"And let us not be weary in well doing: for in due
season we shall reap, if we faint not."
GALATIANS 6:9 KJV

I have always believed that regardless of the circumstances life throws our way, we must strive to do our best in everything we do. It's not about the immediate reward we receive for doing the right things but rather the valuable lessons we learn along the way. You might find yourself thinking, "I've been doing the right things, but it goes unnoticed," or "I don't see how this benefits me." In those moments, please remember that God is watching you and will honor your commitment to Him and your acts of obedience.

Don't worry; continue performing your duties with excellence and integrity, knowing your blessings will follow when you stay the course. It's possible you may not see the reward immediately, but as the Word tells us, we must persist in doing what is right and trust in God's appointed time, not our own. In due season, we will reap the reward. I assure you it will exceed anything you can think of or imagine (Ephesians 3:20). Stay strong in your faith and honor God in all you do.

PRAYER

Father, I have been an obedient and faithful servant. When I grow weary, please give me the strength to remember Your Word and what it promises, for I know it will not return void. Let me stay the course, knowing that if I continue to do what is right, a great harvest will come for the good deeds I have sowed. I believe You will pour me out a blessing I cannot contain (Malachi 3:10). In Jesus' name, we pray. Amen.

REFLECTION

In what ways can you continue to perform your duties with excellence and integrity, even when you don't see immediate rewards?

_____

_____

_____

_____

_____

_____

Reflect on the promise that a great harvest will come for the good deeds you have sowed. How does this promise encourage you to persevere?

_____

_____

_____

_____

_____

_____

_____

DAY 14

SEEK GOD FOR DIRECTION

"We make our plans, but the Lord determines our steps."
PROVERBS 16:9 NLT

Our lives are unique, and we must realize we are only here for an allotted time given to us by our heavenly Father. We could spend time planning and stressing over every detail of our lives, and, in return for our planning, we may receive worry, confusion, and anxiety. How about relaxing, breathing, and being in the present moment?

God orchestrates our every move and places us exactly where we need to be. Flow with life, and don't resist God's plan. Life is a journey of discovery, reflection, and truth. It is meant to be lived to the fullest, with internal guidance from the

Holy Spirit, whom God has sent to be with us. So, before you grow weary on this journey and complain that you're not where you should be, or your life has not turned out how you expected, remember you are not in charge and have no authority over God's plans for you. This may not make sense to you, but our Father is the Alpha and the Omega (Revelation 22:13). He knows your beginning and your end and promises to bring you to a flourishing finish (Philippians 1:6). Trust His plan and remain faithful to the One who shows you the way—better yet—He is the way, the truth and the life (John 14:6). Follow Him. He knows best.

PRAYER

Heavenly Father, thank You for sending Your Holy Spirit to help us navigate this day. Let's hold our plans loosely and hold Your plans tightly. Give us wisdom and the ability to relinquish our control. When we let go and honor You, we know Your will is going to be done in every area of our lives. Thank You for Your guidance. We give You all the praise and glory. In Jesus' name, we pray. Amen.

REFLECTION

Reflect on the statement that God's plan for you will lead to a flourishing finish. How does this perspective inspire you to keep following Him?

_____

_____

_____

_____

_____

_____

_____

_____

How can you actively seek the guidance of the Holy Spirit in making decisions and navigating your life?

_____

_____

_____

_____

_____

_____

_____

_____

DAY 15

THE ARMOR OF GOD

"Put on all of God's armor so that you can stand firm against all strategies of the devil."
EPHESIANS 6:11 NLT

Let's take a moment to reflect on what it means to put on the full armor of God. We are fortunate to serve a God who not only protects us but also equips us with the necessary tools and resources to triumph over our enemies. When life becomes challenging and unfair, such as facing wrongful termination, betrayal from a friend, or a wayward child, we cannot remain silent and succumb to sorrow. Instead, we must rise and combat evil with the powerful Word of God.

Trials and tribulations may come our way, but we can find comfort in knowing that God has already overcome the world, allowing us to have peace in Him (John 16:33). The schemes and tactics of the Devil are no match for our mighty God. When we have faith and trust that He is fighting our battles, and we cover ourselves with the blood of Jesus, we become unstoppable. God always provides protection and strength when we are in distress. Our problems may appear insurmountable, but our God surpasses any obstacle or enemy that tries to stand against us.

God has the ability to turn what the Enemy intended for harm into something good. Just as Daniel emerged unscathed from the lion's den (Daniel 6:16-23), you too will escape from your enemies unharmed. When this happens, remember to offer praise and gratitude to God for His watchful care and protection.

PRAYER

Father, we know darkness must cease in Your presence because You are the light. When we are tempted to do wrong, or someone has wronged us, let us remember to put on our armor to stand up against the Enemy. Please have mercy on us, Father, and let us not be deceived by the Enemy. For we know we are equipped for the battle and will reign victorious. Thank You for Your protection. In Jesus' name, we pray. Amen.

REFLECTION

What does it mean to cover yourself with the blood of Jesus, and how does it provide protection in spiritual battles?

_____

_____

_____

_____

_____

_____

_____

What role does prayer play in putting on the armor of God and seeking His protection in spiritual battles?

_____

_____

_____

_____

_____

_____

_____

_____

DAY 16

BE STRONG

*"Have I not commanded you? Be strong and of good
courage; do not be afraid, nor be dismayed, for the
Lord your God is with you wherever you go."*
JOSHUA 1:9 NKJV

Immense power is within each of us. When I come across
today's scripture, it serves as a reminder not to let my fears
overshadow the truth of who God says I am. As I read these
words, a surge of strength rises within me, overcoming
my weaknesses. It brings me great comfort to know that
God sees us as powerful and courageous beings who can
accomplish all things through Christ who strengthens us
(Philippians 4:13).

Today, I want us to reflect on a task or goal that fear has hindered us from achieving. Now, let us recite this verse and feel God asking us, "Have I not commanded you?" Who are we to feel small or insignificant? Who are we to allow fear to triumph over us? We are far more than our fears and doubts. Fear and doubt do not come from God; they come from the Enemy. We must stand against the Enemy and the negative thoughts that urge us to shrink back and diminish our lights.

God tells us that we are the salt of the earth and the light of the world. He encourages us to let our good deeds shine, glorifying Him in heaven (Matthew 5:13-16). Let us embrace our radiance and confront our fears, knowing that God is with us. He will never leave or forsake us (Deuteronomy 31:8). We do not need to play small; we can dream big and reach for the stars, embracing the infinite possibilities before us.

God has commanded us all to walk in excellence and greatness. When we do so, fear must flee, and our hearts become open to embracing our true potential. Let us step forward, confident in the knowledge that God is by our side, empowering us to become all He has created us to be.

PRAYER

Father, You have promised to be with me wherever I go, and I need You now. I know I can conquer my fears with You on my side. I walk in the light I carry and will achieve the great things You have planned for me. I declare I am made new through Your Word and truth. I will press on toward the mark with confidence and grace. In Jesus' name, we pray. Amen.

REFLECTION

Reflect on a specific area of your life where you have been playing small or shrinking back. How can you start dreaming big and embracing the infinite possibilities before you?

_____

_____

_____

_____

_____

_____

_____

_____

Reflect on the statement that you are the salt of the earth and the light of the world. How does it inspire you to let your good deeds shine and glorify God?

_____

_____

_____

_____

_____

_____

_____

_____

DAY 17

JOY

"Always be joyful. Never stop praying. Be thankful in all circumstances, for this is God's will for you who belong to Christ Jesus."
1 THESSALONIANS 5:16-18 NLT

Joy comes from within and is something no one can take away. True happiness can be experienced when we look within ourselves to see the beauty in the simplicity of life. We may not always feel joyful when life presents challenges, and I can identify with that feeling.

When I lost my grandfather, I was anything but positive; the pain and grief I felt seemed insurmountable. I never thought I would experience such deep pain that would paralyze me in sorrow. The only person who could heal that pain is God. I found joy again by praying fervently and seeking Him. As the scripture says, I can now be thankful for this circumstance because it changed my life and brought me closer to God. I live my life with more purpose.

I could have chosen to sit in my grief and misery, but instead, I decided to keep going and honor God in the way I knew my grandfather would have wanted me to. By simply choosing to get up and be my best each day, I keep my grandfather's legacy alive, and that's something to find joy in. I am incredibly thankful for finding peace and restoration. I'm not sure what has hurt or bothered you, but I want you to change your perspective. Stop focusing on what's wrong and replaying those sad moments. Today, declare that your life will be different. God is doing something new within you. He is restoring your peace and joy. Keep praying, and He will see you through.

PRAYER

Father, I will not let the Enemy steal my joy today. I will remain joyful and optimistic about my circumstances. You know what's best for me, so I will not question You. I choose to be thankful and celebrate the gift of this day, knowing You will take all my sorrows away. Thank You for uplifting me and reminding me to be content in every stage of my life. In Jesus' name, we pray. Amen.

REFLECTION

How has prayer played a role in finding joy and peace in your life?

_____

_____

_____

_____

_____

_____

_____

_____

Reflect on the idea that God is doing something new within you and restoring your peace and joy. How does this inspire hope and optimism?

_____

_____

_____

_____

_____

_____

_____

_____

DAY 18

GOD IS WITH YOU

"When you pass through the waters, I will be with you; And through the rivers, they will not overwhelm you. When you walk through the fire, you will not be scorched, nor will the flame burn you."

ISAIAH 43:2 AMP

Oh, how I love You, Jesus! Every time I read this scripture, I am in awe of the Father's love and protection surrounding me. This scripture brings me comfort amid the chaos in this world. I refuse to let the terror of this world consume me. Instead, I remain anchored in faith, for I know God's plans are to prosper me and give me hope and a future (Jeremiah 29:11).

During the COVID-19 pandemic, the world underwent a profound shift. We were inundated with masks, protective gear, and stay-at-home orders. Every time we turned on the news, we saw the latest outbreaks of COVID-19 and the climbing death toll. This season pushed us all to our limits and caused immense grief for those who lost loved ones in this battle.

In simple terms, the pandemic had devastating effects on our world, and we are still trying to recover, even though we understand the world will never be the same. But through it all, my faith never wavered. I know the God I serve can move mountains, and just as He protected me before, I believe He will protect me again. He did not let the fire of this dreadful virus consume me; instead, He ignited a new fire within me, a fire of compassion for humanity.

If you have gone through adversity, you are here for a reason. God will not let you fall. He will cause your light to shine in the darkness, and you will emerge stronger than before. He is with you in your despair and will not allow any harm to come to you.

PRAYER

Father, thank You for renewing my strength when I am weary. I know You will never leave me or forsake me. I know that no weapon formed against me shall prosper. I rebuke the forces of darkness, for Your light overcomes it. Holy Spirit, I invite You into this atmosphere. Please show me the way, and don't let me fall astray. I will fear no evil, for You comfort me. Father, You are the way, the truth, and the life in which my soul takes rest and delights. In Jesus' name, we pray. Amen.

REFLECTION

In what ways did the COVID-19 pandemic impact your life and the world around you?

_____

_____

_____

_____

_____

_____

_____

_____

How did your faith remain steadfast during the challenges of the pandemic?

_____

_____

_____

_____

_____

_____

_____

_____

_____

DAY 19

FAITH

"For we walk by faith, not by sight."

2 CORINTHIANS 5: 7 NKJV

In life, there are moments when God calls us to move, and our obedience is crucial. Even without all the details, we must act in faith. I was resistant when God urged me to step away from my job. After six years of working for the same company, I became comfortable with its stability. Yet, deep within, I knew God had called me to step out of my comfort zone and utilize the gifts He had bestowed upon me. Although I was filled with fear, I realized I could no longer live an unfulfilled life.

The truth is that I was miserable in my job, and the environment was toxic. The more I resisted, the more challenging it became to endure. Eventually, I made the decision to resign. Even though I didn't have a clear understanding of when or where the next job opportunity would arise, I knew it was the right choice. God had spoken to me years earlier, promising that He had more in store for me. It was now my responsibility to act in faith and pursue my calling.

I am truly walking by faith and not by sight. God birthed this devotional within me, granting me the opportunity to share my experiences and words of hope to encourage others.

You don't have to remain miserable or feel trapped. Instead, take a leap of faith and start walking in your gifts. They will create opportunities and open doors for you (Proverbs 18:16). You are just one decision away from altering the course of your life and impacting future generations. Embrace the newness of this season without fear. God has already ordered your steps and will provide you with the necessary tools and resources to guide you along the way. Witness God's work and experience His favor as you remain obedient.

PRAYER

Father, walking by faith is not always easy, but I trust Your plan for my life. If I am obedient, You will take me places I could never dream of or imagine. I know Your unprecedented favor is in my life, and I believe in explosive blessings in this next season. Thank You for giving me the strength to excel in the discomfort of stepping outside of my comfort zone. For You alone are all I need. In Jesus' name, we pray. Amen.

REFLECTION

Have you ever experienced a moment when you felt a calling from God to make a change or step out of your comfort zone? How did you respond?

_____

_____

_____

_____

_____

_____

_____

_____

Consider a time when you took a leap of faith and witnessed God's work and favor in your life. How did that experience impact your trust and reliance on Him?

_____

_____

_____

_____

_____

_____

_____

_____

DAY 20

FORGIVENESS

"Bear with each other and forgive one another if any of you has a grievance against someone. Forgive as the Lord forgave you."
COLOSSIANS 3:13 NIV

Forgiveness is a universal experience we all encounter in our lives. We understand that it isn't primarily for the person who committed the offense but for ourselves. In the book of Genesis, we witness Joseph's remarkable capacity to forgive despite his brothers' jealousy. They sold him into slavery. However, when famine struck Egypt, Joseph not only forgave his brothers but also provided them with food, shelter, and acceptance in his palace.

Instead of seeking revenge and harboring hatred, Joseph chose love and forgiveness. He reassured his brothers, saying, "Do not be afraid. Am I in the place of God? You intended to harm me, but God intended it for good" (Genesis 50:19). This statement reflects the posture of Joseph's heart—he refused to let unforgiveness overpower his love for his brothers.

Now, I pose a question: "Who has God called you to forgive in your life?" Do not dismiss His instructions and let unforgiveness persist in your heart. Seek God's help in removing any unforgiveness and take action to forgive those who have hurt you. I am confident you can offer others the same grace and forgiveness God extends to you for your own transgressions. Embrace forgiveness so that the process of healing may begin.

PRAYER

Father, please open my heart to forgiveness so I won't carry this heavy burden. I want to experience the healing power of forgiveness. I surrender every offense, and I put it in Your hands. I ask that you forgive my wrongdoings and help me become a better person. Thank You for giving me peace, love, and compassion. In Jesus' name, we pray. Amen.

REFLECTION

Reflect on the grace and forgiveness God extends to you for your transgressions. How does this inspire you to extend forgiveness to others?

_____

_____

_____

_____

_____

_____

_____

How can you demonstrate love, compassion, and acceptance, similar to Joseph's actions, as you extend forgiveness to others?

_____

_____

_____

_____

_____

_____

_____

DAY 21

HUMILITY IN THE BATTLE

*"You armed me with strength for battle; you
humbled my adversaries before me."*

2 SAMUEL 22:40 NIV

You are much stronger than you realize. You are powerful beyond measure. When God combines His supernatural strength with our natural abilities, there are no limits to what we can accomplish. Not only can we put on the full armor of God, but He also provides us with the strength to endure battles and hardships.

Life is not a linear path; it is filled with peaks and valleys, following a natural ebb and flow. Adversity does not discriminate; it knows everyone's address. You cannot outrun or hide from it. Hardships will find you, regardless of the number of good deeds you do or how good of a person you are. You will encounter storms, unfair situations, and betrayal in life.

However, one thing is certain: God has equipped us with everything we need to be victorious in our battles. He can even cause our enemies to bless us when He fights our battles. So, before you react in the flesh and spite someone who has wronged you, consider the power of God. He can take care of your enemies if you entrust them to His hands. What God has planned for your life far surpasses any attack the Enemy may try to use against you.

Do not worry about your enemies or the battles that have plagued you. Regain your joy and allow God to renew your strength and fight your battles. Let us express gratitude to God for His help in easing our hardships.

PRAYER

Father, I know You will strengthen me in this battle. Thank You for Your protection over my life. Thank You for not letting my enemies trample over me. You have allowed me to triumph through adversity and prosper before my enemies. I will count it all joy. In Jesus' name, we pray. Amen.

REFLECTION

How does gratitude help in regaining joy and renewing strength?

_____

_____

_____

_____

_____

_____

_____

_____

How can your personal experiences inspire and encourage others?

_____

_____

_____

_____

_____

_____

_____

_____

_____

DAY 22

GOD'S APPROVAL

*"Am I now trying to win the approval of human
beings, or of God? Or am I trying to please
people? If I were still trying to please people,
I would not be a servant of Christ."*

GALATIANS 1:10 NIV

We have all heard the term "people pleaser" before, and I can relate to the struggles it entails. People pleasing is the tendency to prioritize the needs of others over our own. When we choose to please people, we neglect to establish clear boundaries for ourselves and others, and most importantly, we fail to submit to God first. This way of living can have a detrimental impact on our mental health.

Seeking the approval of others before seeking guidance from God can lead us astray from the path He has designed for us. It can result in pain and setbacks when we are out of alignment with God's will for our lives. However, we must remember that God's approval is all we truly need. I refuse to live my life constantly worrying about the opinions of others, as that only invites ridicule and judgment.

Finding peace in knowing who we are, trusting in God, and seeking His approval brings us joy and freedom. This freedom allows us to embrace our divine destiny and fulfill God's will. I choose to serve God and honor His plan for my life. True fulfillment lies in using the gifts He has bestowed upon us and faithfully following His call.

Do not let rejection or negative opinions from others bring you down. Instead, seek God's approval in everything you do, and you will find the strength to live the life you have always dreamed of.

PRAYER

Father, thank You that I know my worth is found in You, not in the approval of others. I will not allow the opinion of others to distract me from accomplishing Your plans for my life. I will no longer seek to please people. Instead, I choose to serve and honor You because I know who I am and who You have created me to be. In Jesus' name, we pray. Amen.

REFLECTION

How does seeking the approval of others impact your mental health and well-being?

_____

_____

_____

_____

_____

_____

_____

_____

How does knowing your worth in God's eyes protect you from the opinions and judgments of others?

_____

_____

_____

_____

_____

_____

_____

_____

_____

DAY 23

LET YOUR LIGHT SHINE

"In the same way, let your light shine before others, that they may see your good deeds and glorify your Father in heaven."
MATTHEW 5:16 NKJV

There is a radiant light within each of us. What makes this light truly beautiful is the power it holds to express love, compassion, and care. Our lights were never meant to be diminished or obscured. They shine their brightest when we obediently follow God's guidance, perform acts of kindness, and exhibit love toward one another. When we go out of our way to assist those in need or offer prayers for the lost, these acts of goodness are not overlooked. God sees and acknowledges our efforts, and He is pleased with us. Moreover, it brings healing to those we help.

By glorifying God through our submission to His will and using our generosity to aid others, we reflect the image of Christ.

God will abundantly bless you for your acts of kindness and obedience. His blessings will overflow, and you will find that there is not enough room to contain them (Malachi 3:10). So go forth and illuminate the darkness with your light, for you were destined to shine. In the end, as the book of Daniel tells us, "Those who are wise will shine as bright as the sky, and those who lead many to righteousness will shine like the stars forever" (Daniel 12:3).

PRAYER

Father, thank You for the light You shine upon us. May the light we carry be used to magnify and glorify Your mighty name. I want to honor You with my good deeds of love, kindness, generosity, and compassion. Let me live a life that makes You proud and fills me with everlasting joy. In Jesus' name, we pray. Amen.

REFLECTION

What does it mean to express love, compassion, and care through your light?

_____

_____

_____

_____

_____

_____

What blessings can you expect from God for your acts of kindness and obedience?

_____

_____

_____

_____

_____

_____

_____

_____

DAY 24

GOD WILL SUPPLY
YOUR NEEDS

*"And my God will meet all your needs according
to the riches of his glory in Christ Jesus."*
PHILIPPIANS 4:19 NIV

God is longing to shower His goodness upon you. "Look at the birds of the air, for they neither sow nor reap nor gather into barns; yet your heavenly Father feeds them. Are you not more valuable than they?" (Matthew 6:26). If God cares for the birds and provides them with food and nourishment, why do you doubt that He will meet your needs? Your current situation is not a surprise to God. You must believe He will provide you with the necessary resources to navigate this season. His provision will always be timely. He will fulfill your every need, but you must surrender everything to Him. Have faith in your breakthroughs, even when you can't see them.

God loves you deeply! He didn't create you to live a below-average life. No, you were created to live a life of excellence and to walk in your greatness. God will supply your needs and exceed your expectations. Believe that God takes great joy and pleasure in abundantly blessing you. Let's not operate with a mindset of lack but with a heart of fullness, unafraid to ask God for exactly what we need, knowing that we will receive His very best. Release your anxiety and entrust your worries and cares to God, for He cares about you (1 Peter 5:7). God wants you to prosper, and He will meet all your needs.

PRAYER

Father, I surrender every worry and thought that might interfere with my dependence on You. You will meet all my needs and exceed my expectations. I will stay in faith, even when I don't understand Your plan. Thank You for hearing my prayers and renewing my mind. I believe that my breakthrough is coming. In Jesus' name, we pray. Amen.

REFLECTION

What mindset should you have when it comes to God's provision?

_____

_____

_____

_____

_____

_____

_____

_____

What is the significance of comparing God's care for the birds to His care for you?

_____

_____

_____

_____

_____

_____

_____

_____

_____

DAY 25

BE THANKFUL

"Enter his gates with thanksgiving and his courts with praise; give thanks to him and praise his name."

PSALM 100:4 NIV

Thankfulness is a state of being that I intentionally practice every day. I encourage you to do the same. God has breathed life into you and deemed it fitting for you to live another day. Reflect on the times when God rescued you from despair, granted you favorable opportunities, and protected you from danger.

I vividly remember an incident when I was 27 years old. I had a car accident while driving home from a long work-day. My commute was about an hour long, and everything seemed fine until, just five minutes away from home, another motorist hit my vehicle from behind. I heard the loud impact as our cars collided. Initially shocked, I immediately thought, "Thank you, Jesus, I'm okay." I felt the pain from the whiplash, but I was able to leave the scene without significant injuries. On the other hand, the person who hit me suffered life-threatening injuries and had to be airlifted to a nearby hospital. Thankfully, he eventually recovered.

This story tells just one of the countless times when I have felt God's protection in my life. I am immensely grateful that God gave me the grace to navigate through that situation. An overwhelming sense of praise and gratitude fills me when I contemplate God's goodness and mercy.

We give God all glory and offer our heartfelt praises to His mighty name. I will forever remain thankful for His love and protection. Therefore, before you begin your day or the next time you find yourself driving in your car, pause and offer God the praise He rightfully deserves. With the gift of being present today, let us rejoice with a grateful heart and express our thankfulness to our Lord.

PRAYER

Father, as I go through this day, may I have a heart full of thankfulness. I am thankful for Your love, protection, mercy, and grace. I know the things that I have accomplished are only possible with You. I enter Your presence with praise and thanksgiving. Show me ways that I can honor You today. In Jesus' name, we pray. Amen.

REFLECTION

How does practicing thankfulness impact your daily life?

_____

_____

_____

_____

_____

_____

_____

_____

_____

How can you express thankfulness to God throughout your day?

_____

_____

_____

_____

_____

_____

_____

_____

_____

DAY 26

BE OF GOOD CHEER

"A cheerful heart is good medicine,
but a crushed spirit dries up the bones."
PROVERBS 17:22 NIV

Our lives are full of positive and adverse events. We can all agree that positive events bring joy and happiness, but adverse events bring sadness. We have all experienced crushing moments in our lives that have brought down our spirits. The death of a loved one or going through a horrible breakup can deeply cause us sorrow. Yes, it's okay to feel those moments of grief and sadness, but we shouldn't dwell in that place. We must keep moving forward, just as life does.

The only constant in our lives is change. I will rejoice and be glad, for this is the day the Lord has made (Psalm 118:24). When we take time to find joy in our circumstances or discover ways to serve others during our time of suffering, we find the strength to carry on. We realize life is unfair and that we are not in control. So, change your perspective instead of letting a broken spirit take hold of you. Have an attitude of gratitude. Meditate on the positive and find peace in your stillness. Get your joy back. Embrace laughter, the medicine of the soul. You deserve to be happy. There is beauty in every moment, even amid our brokenness. Take time to reflect and heal; you are on the verge of becoming the best version of yourself. Make the choice today to liberate yourself from your sorrows and rise to shine like the star you are!

PRAYER

Father, my spirit is broken, and I'm asking You to restore me to wholeness. When I feel depressed or sad, please give me the courage to stay strong and overcome these negative thoughts. I will move forward cheerful and excited about my future because I know You have an excellent plan for my life. Thank You for giving me hope; I put my trust in You. In Jesus' name, we pray. Amen.

REFLECTION

How can changing our perspective help us overcome a crushed spirit?

_____

_____

_____

_____

_____

_____

_____

What does embracing beauty in every moment, even amid brokenness, mean?

_____

_____

_____

_____

_____

_____

_____

_____

_____

DAY 27

WORDS ARE POWERFUL

*"The tongue has the power of life and death,
and those who love it will eat its fruit."*

PROVERBS 18:21 NIV

Your words matter! What we think about ourselves has the power to determine our destinies. Every day you wake up, make it a priority to speak life into yourself.

We need to fill our spirits with the Word of God and positive affirmations. The Enemy knows when to attack, and if we allow him to take our thoughts captive, it can lead to self-destruction. I refuse to give him this power, knowing that he trembles in fear at the mention of the Almighty God.

Remember, you are more than a conqueror and stronger than you know. With God, all things are possible. Let go of that negative mindset and doubt. Affirm the light you carry within when you look at yourself. Practice speaking positivity over your life. Let's take a moment to recite these affirmations:

- I am talented.
- I am strong.
- I am intelligent.
- I am motivated.
- I am resilient.
- I am confident.
- I am safe.
- I am healthy.
- I am supported.
- I am valued.

You will see God's goodness in your life! Use your words to heal and bring hope into your situation.

PRAYER

Father, thank You for allowing me to recognize the power of what I speak. I declare I will use my words to bless my life and not curse it. I decree health, wholeness, joy, peace, and virtue over my life. Remove the thoughts that hinder me and let Your truth about me prevail. Thank You for keeping me in Your perfect peace. In Jesus' name, we pray. Amen.

REFLECTION

What negative thought patterns or beliefs do you need to let go of to speak life into your circumstances?

_____

_____

_____

_____

_____

_____

How can you intentionally counteract the Enemy's attacks on your thoughts?

_____

_____

_____

_____

_____

_____

_____

Jasmine Chikara

DAY 28

RESIST TEMPTATION

"Submit yourselves before to God. Resist the devil, and he will flee from you."

JAMES 4: 7 KJV

We all face temptations every day. It's something we'll deal with for our entire lives. In this world, God gave us free will that allows us to decide whether we embrace the good or bad things, which is entirely up to us. The Devil has power and can manipulate us into following his schemes if we allow evil to take root in our lives. When you feel tempted to do wrong or engage in behaviors that are not godly, it's essential to stop and pray. If you have doubts about whether something is sinful, it's best to assume it is and ask God for the strength to walk away from that temptation.

One of the first things I notice when I'm under attack or when I act on my selfish desires is that I lose my peace. Anything that disturbs your peace will continue to bother you until you surrender it to God. Acting on our selfish desires leads to self-destruction, but choosing to follow God brings peace and righteousness. By resisting the Devil, we show honor to God and demonstrate our obedience to His Word.

This is challenging. It's written in Scripture, "For everyone has sinned; we all fall short of God's glorious standard" (Romans 3:23). God doesn't expect us to be perfect—only Jesus who came to Earth lived without sin. So, don't be too hard on yourself and beat yourself down when you make mistakes. Instead, acknowledge and confess your sins to the Lord; repent, and He will forgive you. We are all on a journey with God, and everyone's journey will be different. Let's not be quick to judge others. We are all doing the best we can.

The next time temptation strikes, defend yourself by submitting to God and seeking His guidance. Surround yourself with a community of people who encourage you to follow Christ and don't just tell you what you want to hear. By evaluating your choices based on these standards, the Devil will not control you, and you will overcome your selfish desires.

PRAYER

Father, temptation has crossed my path, and I desire to act in my flesh. I am surrendering the desires of my flesh to You because I want to honor You. Please help me recognize the Enemy's schemes and tactics that would try to jeopardize Your plan for my life. I want to live a fruitful and victorious life. So, I lay down my flesh and operate in my spirit. Thank You for giving me the strength to overcome this temptation and renew my mind. In Jesus' name, we pray. Amen.

REFLECTION

What are some specific areas or behaviors in my life where I struggle with temptation and need to submit to God's will?

_____

_____

_____

_____

_____

_____

_____

How can I regularly renew my mind and align my thoughts with God's truth to strengthen my ability to resist temptation?

_____

_____

_____

_____

_____

_____

_____

_____

_____

DAY 29

UNCONDITIONAL LOVE

"Above all, love each other deeply because love covers over a multitude of sins."

I PETER 4:8 NIV

Unconditional love is truly remarkable. My first experience with it was through my mom's love. She has always been there for me, no matter what I've done or how much I've struggled. Her love fills me with hope and encouragement. Many of us have been fortunate to receive this kind of love from our parents. However, I must also mention God's love for us. Thinking about how uniquely He created each of us and how He longs for a deep and loving relationship with us brings me immense joy.

God's love for us is not dependent on circumstances. He invites us to come as we are, even in our brokenness, and He still loves us deeply. Just like parents love their children, our heavenly Father loves us. It's important for us to extend this same love to others. In the Bible, there are two commandments that stand out: "Love the Lord your God with all your heart, soul, and mind... Love your neighbor as yourself" (Matthew 22:36-40). When we love our neighbors as we love ourselves, we bring compassion to a world that often lacks it. We see beyond others' mistakes and approach them with open hearts, ready to forgive and show kindness and mercy. Love has the power to heal, reveal, and soothe our souls. Imagine how beautiful and fulfilling our lives could be if we chose love over hate.

Let's extend love by caring for one another and being more mindful and considerate of each other's feelings. Unconditional love is the bridge that leads to healing, and we all have the opportunity to contribute to bridging that gap.

PRAYER

Father, we thank You for the unconditional love we receive from You daily. We pray that we will extend that same love to others, even when they don't deserve it. With pure intentions, allow the love to flow freely from us so that it might bless those we encounter today. I know that perfect love casts out all fear (1 John 4:18). In Jesus' name, we pray. Amen.

REFLECTION

Have you experienced unconditional love from someone in your life? How did it impact you?

_____

_____

_____

_____

_____

_____

_____

Imagine a world where everyone chose love over hate. How would it impact society?

_____

_____

_____

_____

_____

_____

_____

_____

DAY 30

PERSEVERANCE

"My brethren, count it all joy when you fall into various trials,
knowing that the testing of your faith produces patience."

JAMES 1: 2-3 NKJV

Life is full of challenges and difficulties. Sometimes, when we're following God, we may expect everything to go smoothly and according to our plans, but that's not always the case. Let's face it—life can be challenging. We experience things that are hard to understand, and we may even question if God is there with us. The truth is that God is always by your side. His Word assures us that He will never leave us or abandon us.

I remember when I filed for bankruptcy at the age of 28. It was an unexpected turn in my life, and I didn't know how to recover. I felt a deep sense of shame, and my self-worth hit rock bottom. But God didn't let me stay in that dark place for long. I kept working hard and learned how to manage my finances better. Four years later, I was able to close on my first home. Through perseverance, I stayed committed, and God blessed me in ways I couldn't have imagined.

So, even in your darkest moments, remember that God is with you. He uses those experiences to shape your character and teach you to depend on Him. You can't outrun the goodness of God! God has an incredible plan for your life, and He hasn't forgotten about you. Your faith may be tested, but you can find strength by meditating on God's Word day and night. God loves you and holds you in the palm of His hands. Trust in His plan for your life.

PRAYER

Father, things have happened to me that I don't understand, and if I'm being honest, sometimes those things have made me doubt You. I know You will see me through this trial and bring me out better than before. I trust You, Lord, knowing Your will is going to be done until Your kingdom comes. Thank You for a fresh anointing and for giving me strength for every battle. I will overcome these trials and stand to tell the world about Your glory! In Jesus' name, we pray. Amen.

REFLECTION

How can you support and encourage others who are going through trials and difficulties in their own lives?

_____

_____

_____

_____

_____

_____

_____

_____

Take a moment to pray and surrender your trials and challenges to God, asking Him for perseverance, wisdom, and strength to navigate through them.

_____

_____

_____

_____

_____

_____

_____

_____

DAY 31

NAME CHANGE

"Then God said to Abraham, "Regarding Sarai, your wife—her name will no longer be Sarai. From now on her name will be Sarah. And I will bless her and give you a son from her! Yes, I will bless her richly, and she will become the mother of many nations. Kings of nations will be among her descendants."
GENESIS 17:15-16 NLT

We often resist change, even though it is necessary for our growth. When God elevates us to a new level, it usually requires letting go of something or someone in our lives. This can be difficult. In the Bible, God changed Sarai's name to Sarah before she could give birth to Isaac, the promised child. God knew that her disbelief could hinder her from fulfilling her destiny, so He marked a new beginning in her life by changing her name.

There may be times when we doubt God's call or vision for our lives, just like Sarah did when she laughed at the idea of having a child in her old age (Genesis 18:11-14). But when God ordains something to happen in your life, it will happen, regardless of the obstacles in your path. His plan will always prevail. Maybe you've been doubting and questioning God's purpose for you. It's time to wake up and not be afraid to receive what God has in store for you! You may not need a name change, but you might need to change your location or attitude. You can't carry old habits of disbelief into the next level that God is leading you. God is calling you to rise higher. Don't hesitate; answer His call!

PRAYER

Heavenly Father, we come to You embracing the new things You are doing this season. Reveal to me any areas I need to improve or surrender to You. I am ready for a change and want to live to be the person You created me to be. I believe in unexpected blessings, breakthroughs, and increase in every area of my life. In Jesus' name, we pray. Amen.

REFLECTION

Are there any areas in your life where you have been carrying old habits of disbelief or negativity? How do these habits hinder your growth or ability to fulfill your purpose?

_____

_____

_____

_____

_____

_____

_____

_____

What steps can you take to embrace the new things that God is doing in your life?

_____

_____

_____

_____

_____

_____

_____

_____

ABOUT THE AUTHOR

Jasmine lives in Houston, TX, but she was born in Baton Rouge, LA, and raised in Nashville, TN. She earned her bachelor's degree from Middle Tennessee State University. In her free time, she enjoys activities like writing, reading, focusing on beauty and wellness, and spending quality time with her loved ones. Jasmine is not only an entrepreneur but also a certified life coach. Her passion is to inspire and guide others to embrace their authentic selves by engaging in self-development and connecting with their innermost potential. If you'd like to get in touch with Jasmine, you can reach out to her through her website at jasminechikara.com.

NOTES

Jasmine Chikara

NOTES

_____

_____

_____

_____

_____

_____

_____

_____

_____

_____

_____

_____

_____

_____

_____

_____

_____

_____

_____

_____

_____

_____

_____

_____

_____

_____

_____

NOTES

Jasmine Chikara

NOTES

NOTES

Jasmine Chikara

NOTES

www.ingramcontent.com/pod-product-compliance
Lightning Source LLC
Chambersburg PA
CBHW060326130626
46553CB00003B/927